# *Discovering You*

# *Discovering You*

*A Guide to Finding Your Inner Peace and Power*

Brooklyn Goffnett

Discovering You™

Brooklyn Goffnett

Original Copyright © 2024

All Rights Reserved

ISBN: 9798218436858

No part of this book may be reproduced, stored in a retrieval system, or transmitted in any form or by any means, mechanical, electronic, photocopying, recording, or otherwise, without prior written permission of the author, except for brief quotations in a review or article. Unauthorized reproduction or distribution of this book, or any portion of it, may result in severe civil and criminal penalties and will be prosecuted to the maximum extent possible under the law. For permissions requests, write to the author at: brooklyngoffnett@protonmail.com

The author of this book is not a medical professional and does not provide medical advice or prescribe treatments. The information provided is for general purposes only and should not be used as a substitute for professional medical advice, diagnosis, or treatment. Always seek the advice of your physician or another qualified healthcare provider with any questions regarding a medical condition, and never disregard professional medical advice or delay seeking it because of something you have read in this book. The author and publisher assume no responsibility for your actions or any consequences resulting from the use of the information in this book, and they disclaim any liability for any loss, damage, or injury caused directly or indirectly by its contents.

# *Table of Contents*

Forward

Preface

Cultivating Unconditional Self-Love

Embracing Authentic Self-Acceptance

Discovering Your Unique Beauty: Nurturing Self-Love in a World of Comparison

Embracing Vulnerability and Authenticity

Cultivating Inner Strength Through Resilience

Harnessing the Power of Mindfulness and Presence

Setting Boundaries and Overcoming People-Pleasing Behavior

Unleashing the Power Within: Manifesting Your Reality

Creating a Life of Purpose and Meaning

Illuminating Your Path Ahead

Message from the Author

## *Forward*

I would have never in a million years thought I'd be writing and publishing a book! Not even a year ago, I was frustrated with life, trying to find a path that felt genuine and in line with who I am. I felt stuck and hopeless, trapped in a relentless cycle that offered no escape. Then, one day, I realized that the reason I was so unhappy with life was that I had no idea what I wanted my life to look like. I was so focused on achieving success that I neglected to consider my true life's purpose. I didn't know who I was, or what my real desires were. That's when I decided to start dedicating time to understanding myself at a deeper level and figure out what I truly wanted out of life. As I plunged deeper into self-exploration and began to truly understand who I was, I noticed a remarkable transformation in my life. Gradually, I began making more and more positive decisions that ultimately served me and my greater purpose. I stopped wasting time on things that did not benefit me and began focusing on my passions and goals. I felt like my head was finally above water, and I could see clearly for the first time in a long time.

It was during this period of clarity that I realized many others were experiencing the same feelings of hopelessness and stagnation that I once did. This realization inspired me to share my story and help guide others on their own path of self-discovery.

My hope is; by writing this book, I can help others find the inner peace, self-love, and true freedom that I now feel. I believe everyone deserves a life that brings genuine happiness, and to achieve that, you must begin by loving yourself. So, take the leap of faith, and let's explore your innermost desires and fears together, so you can break free from the chains of self-doubt and embrace the limitless potential that lies within you. Remember, you are worthy of love and happiness, and it all starts with loving yourself first. I sincerely hope this book helps you as much as it helped me. If I can inspire even one person to start their own path of self-discovery and transformation, then every word I've written will have been worth it. Thank you for joining me on this journey. Here's to finding our true selves and living the lives we are meant to live.

# *Preface*

To anyone who's ever felt trapped in their own thoughts, convinced that growth and happiness were meant for others but somehow just out of reach for you-then look no further, because you just found the book that has the potential to change your life. And before you scoff and throw this book to the side, why don't you choose a different path this time? Instead of choosing pessimism and listening to your self-doubt, just this one time, allow yourself to believe in change and believe that you are worthy enough to live a life that makes you proud and gives you happiness.

Within these pages, you will find the tools and guidance you've been searching for, that will help you break free from the chains of self-doubt and insecurity. You will learn how to cultivate a mindset of abundance and self-love, allowing you to finally step into your full potential and create a life that truly brings you joy. So, dear reader, I invite you to open your heart and mind as we begin on this transformative journey together.

While you may recognize your potential and ability for greatness, you might find yourself lacking a clear path forward. Here, we'll look at the skill of developing unconditional self-love and how to incorporate it into our daily lives through practical habits and new ways of thinking. This will help shift the idea of self-love from a distant objective to a real attainable goal. We'll explore the transformative power of embracing authenticity, seeing every challenge not as a setback but as an opportunity for growth. Together, we'll discover the beauty in vulnerability, the strength in resilience, and the freedom in letting go of societal expectations to truly embrace who we are.

Each chapter serves as a steppingstone on your journey towards becoming the best version of yourself. We will explore practical exercises and introspective reflections aimed at shattering the chains of self-doubt and fear and replace them with confidence, clarity, and a profound sense of purpose. Whether it's overcoming mental blocks or manifesting your dreams, this book will serve as a guide to help you rediscover your inner strength and unleash your true potential.

View this book as a personal invitation to break free from your mental slump and step into an era of enlightenment, self-awareness, and personal development. This book is written for you, in hopes you find it as an inspiration and sign that you deserve more than you're giving yourself. Within these pages, I hope you find the courage, inspiration, and resources you need to start the most fulfilling journey of all – becoming the best version of yourself. So, take a deep breath, turn the page, and let's set off on this adventure together. Your future self awaits, and the journey to meet them is now. I promise you; your future self will thank you for the effort and the love you are about to give yourself.

# Chapter 1:
# Cultivating Unconditional Self-Love

In the journey of life, the first and most crucial step toward fulfillment and happiness is cultivating unconditional self-love. This chapter guides you through the process of learning to authentically appreciate yourself for all that you are. Through practical exercises and introspective techniques, you will discover the inherent value you possess within, embracing your unique qualities, talents, and experiences.

Self-love is the foundation of your journey to fulfillment and happiness. It's about appreciating yourself for who you are and taking actions that support your growth in every aspect of life. This appreciation means caring deeply for yourself, forgiving your mistakes, and prioritizing your well-being and happiness.

*Discovering Self-Love*

Self-love is the cornerstone of a joyful, abundant life. It's about recognizing your worth, honoring your journey, and acknowledging your strengths and weaknesses with compassion and understanding. To begin your journey, start with a simple but powerful exercise:

## Exercise: Self-Love Affirmation

Begin each day with affirmations that reinforce your commitment to self-love. Here are a few to get you start:

"I am worthy of love and happiness."
"I accept myself unconditionally."
"My challenges help me grow and become stronger."

_____
_____
_____
_____
_____
_____
_____
_____
_____
_____
_____
_____

Repeat these affirmations every morning to set a positive tone for your day. A good time to do these affirmations is either right when you wake up, or you can say them to yourself in the mirror when you're getting around for the day. It's important that you really focus on believing in what you say, it isn't nearly as effective if you are just mindlessly reciting them with no thought or focus.

*Exercise: Mirror Conversation*

The Mirror Conversation Exercise is another great way to learn to have more compassion with yourself. It's harder to be mean to yourself when you're looking yourself in the eyes. Try this exercise next time you aren't feeling the best about yourself.

~ Stand in front of a mirror, look into your eyes, and speak words of love and encouragement to yourself. Begin with, "I love you, and I accept you exactly as you are."

~ Mention at least three qualities you appreciate about yourself. These can be related to your personality, achievements, or physical attributes.

~ Repeat this exercise daily, each time acknowledging different qualities.

Words of Love and Encouragement to Myself:

_____
_____
_____
_____
_____
_____
_____
_____
_____
_____
_____

If you are still having a hard time with the exercise, you can tape a childhood picture of yourself to the corner of the mirror. Whenever you want to hate on yourself or you start picking out your flaws, look at that picture and think, would you say these things to her? Would you want to put this negativity on her?

*Embracing Your Entire Being*

Unconditional self-love requires embracing all facets of your being, including the parts you may find challenging to accept. This acceptance does not mean resignation; it means acknowledging your current state while understanding that you are a work in progress, always capable of growth and change. By recognizing and loving all parts of yourself, you can cultivate a sense of inner peace and fulfillment that comes from knowing you are worthy of love just as you are.
Embracing self-love allows you to navigate life's challenges with resilience and compassion towards yourself.

*Exercise: Journaling Your Journey*

~ Start a self-love journal. Each day, write down three things you did well or three things you like about yourself.

~ Reflect on your challenges and write about how they have contributed to your growth. Recognize that every experience, positive or negative, has shaped you.

## Radiating Love Outward

When you fill yourself with love, it naturally overflows and touches the lives of others. Your self-love becomes a beacon of light, inspiring those around you to commence on their own journeys of self-appreciation.

---
*Exercise: Acts of Kindness*

---

- Each day, perform an act of kindness for yourself and for someone else. This could be as simple as giving yourself time to enjoy a hobby or sending a supportive message to a friend.

~ Notice how these acts of kindness, both given and received, enhance your sense of self-love and connection with others. Journal your journey and experiences here:

_____
_____
_____
_____
_____
_____
_____
_____
_____
_____
_____
_____
_____
_____

## Overcoming Obstacles to Self-Love

There are a lot of things that can get in the way of self-love: past traumas, societal pressures, and the habit of comparing ourselves to others. When we become stuck in a cycle of discontentment with ourselves, it can become hard to find the motivation to do anything. You choose to listen to the voice of fear and doubt, instead of believing in yourself and feeling excited that you will accomplish what you set your mind to. So how can you change this way of thinking? You have to make a conscious effort to change your mindset, and change the way you see yourself, and you must be willing to face and accept your vulnerabilities.

A key step in this process is adjusting your habits to foster self-appreciation. For instance, limiting social media use can significantly reduce unhealthy comparisons. By focusing more on your personal achievements and goals, you cultivate a deeper appreciation for your unique path.

---

*Exercise: The Comparison Detox*

---

- For one week, consciously avoid comparing yourself to others, whether in real life or on social media. Whenever you catch yourself in the act of comparison, redirect your focus to something you appreciate about yourself, or go do an activity that will get you closer to your goals (focus on what you can do/ have, not on what you wish you were/ wish you had). Journal your journey and experiences here:

_____
_____
_____
_____
_____
_____

## *Integrating Self-Love into Daily Life*

Making self-love a daily practice is essential for it to become a natural part of your being. Self-love isn't just about loving what you see in the mirror; it's about loving yourself enough to do what's best for you, even when you don't want to. It's about self-reflection and being honest with yourself about the choices you make, whether good or bad, and how they affect your life. You also have to put yourself first and make sure your own needs are met. You can do this by setting boundaries, practicing self-care, and making choices that reflect your self-worth.

*Exercise: Self Love in Action*

Identify one self-love action you can take each day this week. This could be as simple as taking a night for some self-care so you can feel attractive and confident, or you could splurge on yourself and buy some new clothes or shoes (never underestimate the power of a new outfit). Whatever you do to refuel your love meter, take the time afterwards to reflect on how each action made you feel and how it contributed to your sense of self-love.

_____

_____

_____

_____

_____

_____

_____

_____

_____

_____

**Reflective Questions:**

1. What does self-love mean to you, and how can you cultivate more of it in your life?
2. Think of a time when you were hard on yourself. How could you have approached this situation differently with self-love? How will you show yourself more love and patience next time you're in a similar situation?
3. Identify a self-love practice you want to adopt.
4. What steps will you take to integrate it into your life?

Cultivating unconditional self-love is a journey that requires patience and practice. By engaging in these exercises and embracing your inherent worth, you set the foundation for a life filled with joy, self-acceptance, and fulfillment.

Remember, the love you seek from the world starts with the love you give to yourself.

## Chapter 2:
## *Embracing Authentic Self-Acceptance*

Beginning the journey of self-acceptance is like unlocking the door to your inner universe, one that's full of potential for growth, happiness, and peace. This chapter is your guide to embracing and loving the real you, flaws and all. Through self-reflection, exercises, and a commitment to personal truth, you'll learn to appreciate your uniqueness and live with a profound sense of inner peace.

*Self-Acceptance: The Heart of Personal Freedom*

Self-acceptance is the act of recognizing and embracing all aspects of yourself-your strengths, your vulnerabilities, and everything in between. It's about making peace with who you are at your core and freeing yourself from the shackles of self-doubt and societal expectations.

Self-acceptance is a deeply personal and transformative act. It's not just about acknowledging your strengths and vulnerabilities; it's about wholeheartedly embracing them as essential components of your unique identity. This journey towards self-acceptance is about tuning into your inner voice and silencing the external noises that dictate who you should be. It's about standing firm in your truth, even when the world tries to sway you.

Imagine walking a path in a dense forest-the forest representing the world with its numerous expectations, opinions, and judgments. Your task is not to follow the well-trodden paths laid out by others but to carve your own, guided by the compass of your true self. This may mean stepping into underbrush and facing the unknown with courage, but every step forward is a step towards authentic living.

## *Embracing All That You Are*

Recognizing and accepting all facets of oneself is like staring at a mosaic-each piece, no matter how bright or dull, fits together perfectly to form a beautiful whole. Your strengths shine brightly, illuminating your path and guiding you forward. Your vulnerabilities, on the other hand, are not flaws but facets that add depth and texture to your being. Together, they form the complete picture of who you are.

Self-acceptance means making peace with your past, your mistakes, and the parts of you that you've struggled to love. It's about understanding that growth and imperfection are part of being human. When you free yourself from the shackles of self-doubt and societal expectations, you grant yourself the freedom to be your true self, unapologetically.

*Exercise: A Guided Reflection*

Take a moment to reflect on your journey so far. Think about the times when you felt pressured to conform to someone else's idea of perfection. How did it feel? Now, consider the moments when you were true to yourself, despite the fear of judgment or rejection. There's a sense of liberation in those moments, isn't there?

Here's a guided reflection to deepen your practice of self-acceptance:

- Find a quiet space where you can be alone with your thoughts.

- Take a few deep breaths and center yourself in the present moment.

- Reflect on your strengths. What are you proud of? When do you feel the most confident / most in your flow state, and what parts of you are responsible for you feeling this way? Allow yourself to feel gratitude for these qualities.

- Now, gently turn your attention to your vulnerabilities. Acknowledge them without judgment. Consider how they have contributed to your growth and understanding of yourself and reflect on how you can transform these aspects of yourself into strengths (ex. Don't see your failures as setbacks, see them as an opportunity to better understand others and yourself. And look at the outcome of you overcoming these obstacles. You would have never grown the way you have without them, so they were necessary in your life)

- Visualize yourself embracing all parts of your being, offering compassion, and understanding to each aspect. If you're a visual person, you can write down all your strengths and vulnerabilities down and reflect on them throughout the day in a positive and grateful light.

- Affirm to yourself, "I am worthy of love and acceptance, exactly as I am."

Strengths:

_____
_____
_____
_____
_____

_____
_____

Weaknesses:

_____
_____
_____
_____
_____
_____

_____

By integrating this practice into your life, you'll begin to notice a shift in how you view yourself and the world around you. Self-acceptance doesn't happen overnight, but each step taken in authenticity brings you closer to the freedom and joy of being your true self.

*Exercise: Reflections of Self*

Take a moment each day to reflect on your thoughts and feelings. Ask yourself:

- What am I truly passionate about?
- What strengths do I possess that I'm proud of?
- How can I accept and learn from my weaknesses?

Write down your reflections to foster a deeper understanding and acceptance of your true self.

*Navigating the Path of Self-Discovery*

The path to self-acceptance is unique for everyone and requires courage to confront and embrace your true self. It's about acknowledging your imperfections and still choosing to celebrate your essence.

*Exercise: Embracing Imperfection*

~ List three imperfections or weaknesses you've struggled to accept.

~ Next to each, write a positive aspect or how it has contributed to your personal growth.

~ Reflect on how accepting these parts of yourself can lead to greater self-compassion and freedom.

_____
_____
_____
_____
_____
_____
_____
_____
_____
_____
_____
_____
_____
_____

## The Power of Authenticity

Living authentically means aligning your actions with your true self. It's about making decisions based on what genuinely matters to you, not what others expect of you.

*Exercise: Decision Audit*

~ Think about a recent decision you made. Was it true to your desires, or were you influenced by others?

~ Going forward, how can you ensure your decisions reflect your authentic self?

_____
_____
_____
_____
_____
_____
_____
_____
_____
_____
_____
_____
_____
_____
_____

## Building a Foundation of Self-Acceptance

Cultivating self-acceptance is an ongoing process that enriches your life, relationships, and sense of well-being. It requires mindfulness, dedication, and the willingness to see yourself through a lens of compassion.

---
### Exercise: Acts of Self-Acceptance
---

~ Choose one act of self-acceptance to practice daily. This could be affirming your worth, setting boundaries to protect your energy, or pursuing a passion that lights you up.

~ Reflect on how each act enhances your relationship with yourself and with others.

**Reflective Questions:**

1. What are the biggest barriers to self-acceptance you've faced, and how can you overcome them?
2. How does embracing your authentic self-change the way you interact with the world?
3. Identify one step you can take this week to live more authentically. How will this action bring you closer to true self-acceptance?

Finding your true authentic self is not just a destination; it's a journey that unfolds with every choice you make to be true to yourself and your beliefs. It's about recognizing your worth, understanding your unique journey, and acknowledging your strengths and weaknesses with love.

This chapter has outlined the steps for you to take on this transforming journey, including the tools and reflections required to cultivate a profound, loving acceptance of who you are. Remember, the path to personal fulfillment and happiness is built on the bedrock of self-acceptance.

# Chapter 3:

## Discovering Your Unique Beauty

### Nurturing Self-Love in a World of Comparison

In an era where social media and societal standards often dictate the norms of beauty and success, it's easy to lose sight of our inherent, unique worth. This chapter is an invitation to start your path of self-exploration, and to begin your personal journey of discovering and embracing your own unique beauty-a beauty that transcends physical appearances and societal benchmarks.

*Understanding Your Unique Beauty*

Each individual is a masterpiece of unique experiences, thoughts, emotions, and physical attributes. Unlike the fleeting standards of beauty that change with time and culture, your unique beauty is timeless and irreplaceable. It's a combination of your spirit, your resilience, your kindness, and every little quirk that makes you, you.

Before diving into the practices aimed at uncovering your unique beauty, it's essential to understand that beauty is not a one-size-fits-all concept. It's multifaceted and encompasses more than what meets the eye. True beauty reflects your inner self-your values, your passions, and your ability to stand in your truth.

## Exercise: Beauty Beyond the Mirror

This exercise is designed to help you shift your focus from external appearances to the qualities that embody your inner beauty.

~ Reflect on experiences where you felt most alive or appreciated. What qualities were you expressing?

~ Write down instances when you overcame challenges of self-doubt/ not feeling good enough. How did these experiences highlight your unique strengths?

_____
_____
_____
_____
_____
_____
_____
_____
_____
_____

### Shifting the Focus from Comparison to Self-Appreciation

The compulsion to compare ourselves to others is a natural human inclination, but it inevitably leads to feelings of inadequacy, causing us to undermine our self-esteem and worth. Understanding the psychology behind comparison- the innate desire to assess our standing in relation to others-can be the first step toward breaking free from its grip. This section discusses ways to channel our comparative impulses toward self-reflection and appreciation, improving self-image.

## Exercise: Gratitude/or Uniqueness

~ Contemplate the qualities or achievements you've accomplished in life and consider how your life would be different without them.

~ This reflection is aimed at fostering a deep appreciation for your journey and the unique attributes that you bring to the world.

___

### Creating a Self-Love Routine

Developing a self-love routine is about setting aside intentional time for self-care and reflection, creating a space where you can connect with and celebrate your unique essence. This section explores the importance of routines in reinforcing self-worth and how personalized routines can serve as a powerful antidote to external pressures and comparisons.

Exercise: Designing Your Self-Love Routine

~ Consider activities that resonate with your soul, quiet the mind and bring you joy. This could be as simple as a morning walk, journaling, or meditating/ practicing mindfulness.

_____

_____

_____

_____

_____

_____

_____

~ Carve out time throughout your week to practice these activities. Use this time as constructive time to refuel your charge and rejuvenate yourself in a new sense of confidence and freedom. The aim is to create a sacred space and time where you can engage with yourself in a loving and accepting manner, reinforcing your sense of inherent beauty and worth.

*Overcoming Social Media's Influence*

In our digital age, social media is a double-edged sword. It connects us, inspires us, and offers a platform for self-expression. Yet, it's also a breeding ground for comparison, often showcasing an idealized version of life that can distort our perception of reality. This discrepancy between the curated lives we see online, and our own experiences can lead to feelings of inadequacy and a diminished sense of self-love.

## The Comparison Trap

Social media platforms are designed to engage us, keeping us scrolling through endless feeds of highlights from others' lives. These snippets, however polished and perfect they may seem, are just that-fragments of a much larger picture. It's essential to remind ourselves that what we're seeing is often a curated selection of the best moments, carefully chosen and edited to portray an ideal, not the full spectrum of everyday life.

### Shifting Your Perspective

Acknowledge the Partial Picture: Start by acknowledging that social media profiles are not comprehensive reflections of life. They are the highlight reels, not the behind-the-scenes. This recognition is the first step toward detaching your self-worth from comparisons to these chosen snippets.

Cultivate Mindfulness: When browsing social media, practice mindfulness by being aware of how certain content makes you feel. If you notice feelings of inadequacy or envy, take a moment to step back and reflect on why this content triggers these emotions. Use these feelings as signals to re-evaluate how you engage with social media.

Limit Exposure: Consider setting boundaries around your social media use. This could mean limiting your daily usage, having specific times of the day when you don't check social media, or even taking periodic breaks from platforms that trigger negative comparisons.

*Exercise: Social Media Intention Setting*

~ Take a moment to reflect on your social media habits and how they impact your feelings about yourself. Identify which aspects of social media contribute to feelings of comparison or inadequacy.

_____
_____
_____
_____
_____
_____

~ Set clear intentions for your social media use. This might involve unfollowing accounts that don't contribute to your well-being, following more accounts that inspire and uplift you, or changing your routine to include social media-free times or activities.

<u>Creating a Positive Digital Environment</u>

Curate Your Feed: Actively curate your social media feed to include content that inspires, educates, and uplifts you.
Follow accounts that promote body positivity, mental health, personal growth, and authentic living. Seeing more realistic and varied representations of life can help counteract the negative effects of comparison.

Engage Actively: Shift from passive scrolling to active engagement. Use social media to connect genuinely with others, share your own stories authentically, and support content that aligns with your values. By contributing positively to the digital community, you reinforce your sense of purpose and belonging.

**Reflective Questions:**

1. Reflect on the moments when comparison has overshadowed your ability to appreciate your unique beauty. How can you redirect those thoughts toward self-appreciation?
2. How does my current social media consumption affect my perception of myself and my life?
3. What changes can I make to my social media habits to foster a healthier relationship with these platforms?
4. How can I use social media in a way that aligns with my values and supports my well-being? The goal is to curate a social media experience that supports rather than detracts from your journey of self-love and appreciation.

By adopting a more mindful and intentional approach to social media, you can begin to liberate yourself from the cycle of comparison and inadequacy. Remember, the key to nurturing self-love in a world of comparison is to focus on your journey, celebrate your unique path, and remember that true worth cannot be measured by likes or follows.

As you journey through this chapter and beyond, remember that discovering and nurturing your unique beauty is a deeply personal and empowering process. It's about celebrating yourself in all your complexity, embracing your individuality, and cultivating a loving relationship with yourself that stands resilient in the face of external comparisons and pressures.

## Chapter 4:
## Embracing Vulnerability and Authenticity

In a world that often values strength and certainty, embracing vulnerability and authenticity can seem counterintuitive. Yet, it is through embracing our true selves, with all our fears, hopes, and imperfections, that we find genuine connection, courage, and a path to personal fulfillment. This chapter delves into the importance of vulnerability and authenticity, challenging you to live openly and wholeheartedly.

*The Strength in Vulnerability*

Vulnerability is not a weakness but a profound strength. It's the courage to show up and be seen, to share our true selves, and to engage deeply with life, even when there are no guarantees. Vulnerability is the birthplace of love, belonging, joy, courage, empathy, and creativity. It's in those moments when we feel most exposed that we have the opportunity to forge the deepest connections and to grow.

*Practices for Embracing Vulnerability*

Share Your Story: Open up about your experiences, thoughts, and feelings with *trusted* individuals. Sharing your story can be liberating and can deepen your connections with others.

Practice Self-Compassion: Treat yourself with kindness and understanding, especially when you feel vulnerable.
Remember that being vulnerable is a sign of courage, not weakness.

Set Boundaries: Embracing vulnerability doesn't mean oversharing or ignoring your comfort levels. Setting healthy boundaries is an integral part of being authentic and protecting your emotional well-being.

### Living Authentically in Different Aspects of Life

In Relationships: Show up as your true self in your relationships. Honest and open communication fosters deeper connections and mutual respect.

At Work: Bring your whole self to work. Letting your true personality shine can lead to more meaningful engagement with your work and colleagues.

In Personal Growth: Pursue activities and goals that align with your authentic self. Living in accordance with your values and interests leads to greater satisfaction and fulfillment.

### Overcoming the Fear of Vulnerability

Fear of rejection, judgment, or failure often holds us back from being vulnerable and authentic. Recognizing that these fears are common can help us feel less isolated in our experiences. By taking small, courageous steps toward openness, we can gradually overcome these fears and discover the empowering freedom that comes with living authentically.

*Exercise: The Vulnerability Step Ladder*

The purpose of this exercise is to create a series of progressively challenging steps that encourage you to face your fear of rejection and vulnerability. By taking incremental risks, you can slowly build your comfort with vulnerability, reducing the fear associated with it.

*Step 1: Self-Reflection*

Write down specific situations where you fear rejection or feel vulnerable. This could include expressing an unpopular opinion, asking for help, or sharing personal stories or feelings. Next to each situation, rate your fear on a scale of 1 to 10 (where 1 is minimal fear and 10 is extreme fear).

_____
_____
_____
_____
_____
_____
_____
_____
_____
_____
_____
_____
_____
_____
_____

*Step 2: Create Your Vulnerability Ladder*

Based on your self-reflection, create a "vulnerability ladder" with steps ordered from least to most frightening. For example, your ladder may start with sharing an opinion on a non-controversial topic with a friend (lower rung) and lead up to expressing your feelings to someone you care about (higher rung).

*Step 3: Take the First Step*

Begin with the lowest rung on your **ladder**, the situation that induces the **least** fear. Plan a specific action you can take to face this fear. For instance, if your first step involves sharing an opinion, choose a safe and appropriate context to express it. After taking action, reflect on the experience. Write down what **happened,** how you felt before, during, and after, and what you learned from the experience.

*Step 4: Gradual Progression*

Once you feel comfortable with the outcome of the first step, move on to the next rung on your ladder. Repeat the process of planning, action, and reflection. Continue this progression, allowing yourself to feel and acknowledge the fear without letting it deter you. With each step, your confidence and comfort with vulnerability will grow.

*Step 5: Reflect and Celebrate*

After completing several steps, or even the entire ladder, take time to reflect on your journey. Acknowledge the growth and progress you've made in overcoming your fear of rejection. Celebrate your bravery and the steps you've taken toward embracing vulnerability. Recognize that each act of courage, no matter how small, is a victory in your personal development.

_____
_____
_____
_____
_____
_____
_____
_____
_____
_____
_____
_____
_____
_____
_____
_____
_____

By engaging in the Vulnerability Step Ladder exercise, you can methodically confront and diminish your fear of rejection, gaining confidence in your ability to be vulnerable and authentic. This process not only reduces fear but also enhances your resilience, deepening your connections with others and enriching your life experience.

*Key Reminders:*

Progress at your own pace. There's no rush to complete your vulnerability ladder. What matters is consistent, gradual exposure to your fears.

Embrace setbacks as learning opportunities. Not every attempt will be successful, and that's okay. Each experience provides valuable insights.

- Support is crucial. Share your goals with a trusted friend or family member who can encourage you and provide feedback.

**Reflective Questions:**

1. What does being vulnerable mean to me? How can I incorporate more vulnerability into my life?
2. In which areas do I struggle to be authentic, and what small changes can I make to express my true self?
3. How can embracing vulnerability and authenticity lead to a more fulfilling life?

Embracing vulnerability and authenticity is a powerful journey toward self-discovery and connection. It challenges us to confront our fears, to live according to our deepest truths, and to engage with the world from a place of openness and strength. By choosing to be vulnerable and authentic, we open ourselves up to a life rich with connection, growth, and true fulfillment.

# Chapter 5:

## Cultivating Inner Strength Through Resilience

Resilience is the capacity to recover quickly from difficulties; it's about bending instead of breaking under pressure and coming back stronger than before. In the journey of self-improvement and manifestation, resilience is a cornerstone of success. It allows us to maintain our course in the face of setbacks, learn from our experiences, and continue to grow.

### The Importance of Resilience

Life is unpredictable and often challenging. Resilience equips us with the ability to navigate these challenges without losing sight of our goals. It's not about avoiding difficulties but facing them head-on, learning, and adapting. Resilient individuals are characterized by their perseverance, optimism, and flexibility. They view challenges as opportunities for growth rather than insurmountable obstacles.

### Building Blocks of Resilience

Resilience is built on several key components, including self-awareness, self-regulation, optimism, and support networks. Self-awareness allows us to understand our reactions to stress and adversity. Self-regulation helps us manage those reactions effectively. Optimism ensures we maintain a hopeful outlook, and support networks provide the external encouragement and perspective needed to navigate tough times.

*Strategies for Enhancing Resilience*

Embrace a Growth Mindset: Believe in your ability to learn and grow from every situation. View challenges as opportunities to expand your skills and understanding.

Develop Problem-Solving Skills: Approach problems with a calm and strategic mindset. Break them down into manageable parts and look for creative solutions.

Cultivate Self-Care: Resilience is fueled by physical and emotional well-being. Ensure you're taking care of your body with proper nutrition, exercise, and rest. Nurture your emotional health through mindfulness practices, hobbies, and spending time with loved ones.

Build Supportive Relationships: Surround yourself with people who encourage and support you. Being able to share your experiences and gain perspective from others is invaluable in building resilience.

Learn to Adapt: Flexibility is a key component of resilience. Be open to change and willing to adjust your plans based on new information or circumstances.

Resilience is not just about surviving life's challenges but thriving amid them. It involves seeing obstacles not as barriers but as steppingstones to greater growth and achievement. This chapter will explore how embracing challenges as opportunities and maintaining a positive self-esteem and outlook can transform the way we navigate life's ups and downs, ensuring we remain undeterred in our pursuit of goals, even in the face of repeated setbacks.

## Embracing Obstacles as Opportunities

The way we perceive challenges significantly impacts our ability to overcome them. Viewing difficulties as opportunities requires a shift in mindset-a conscious choice to seek out the lessons and growth potential in every situation. This approach not only makes us more resilient but also opens us up to possibilities we might not have considered otherwise.

### Strategies for Positive Reframing

Seek the Lesson: Every challenge comes with a lesson. Ask yourself, "What can I learn from this experience?" Focusing on the takeaway rather than the setback shifts your perspective from victim to learner.

Celebrate Small Wins: Progress is progress, no matter how small. Celebrate every step forward, as these victories build momentum and reinforce your ability to overcome challenges.

Visualize Success: Keep your eyes on the prize. Visualize overcoming the obstacle and achieving your goal. This positive imagery encourages perseverance and keeps you motivated.

## Exercise: Positive Reframing

Practice reframing challenges into opportunities, shifting your perspective to see the potential for growth in adversity.

Identify a Challenge: Think of a recent challenge or setback you've faced. Write it down in detail, including how it made you feel and why it felt like a setback.

_____
_____
_____
_____
_____
_____
_____
_____

Seek the Opportunity: Now, take a moment to reframe this challenge. Ask yourself: What can I learn from this situation? How can this challenge make me stronger, wiser, or more compassionate? Is there a hidden opportunity here for a new direction, skill, or relationship?

_____
_____
_____
_____
_____
_____
_____
_____

Write the Reframe: Write down the challenge again, but this time include the opportunities you've identified. Phrase it in a way that highlights these opportunities, transforming the narrative from a tale of setback to one of growth.

_____
_____
_____
_____
_____
_____
_____
_____

Reflect: Reflect on this reframing process. How does changing your perspective on the challenge change how you feel about it? Can you apply this reframing technique to other areas of your life?

_____
_____
_____
_____
_____
_____
_____
_____
_____

## Maintaining Positive Self-Esteem and Attitude

Your self-esteem and attitude play a pivotal role in how you face challenges. Maintaining a positive self-image and outlook is essential, especially when you find yourself starting over or trying multiple times to achieve your goals.

### Techniques for Building Self-Esteem and Positivity

Affirm Your Worth: Regularly affirm your value and capabilities. Use positive affirmations to reinforce your self-worth and remind yourself of your strengths and achievements.

Surround Yourself with Positivity: Engage with supportive and uplifting people. Limit exposure to negativity, whether from individuals or media, that can erode your self-esteem and outlook.

Embrace Self-Compassion: Treat yourself with the same kindness and understanding you would offer a friend. Acknowledge that setbacks are part of the journey and don't define your worth or potential.

*Exercise: Self-Esteem Builder*

Let's strengthen your self-esteem by recognizing your achievements, qualities, and growth, reinforcing a positive self-image even in the face of setbacks.

Write down three personal qualities you love about yourself. These can be character traits, skills, or areas where you've shown growth. Be specific and honest.

_____

_____
_____
_____
_____

_____
_____

For each quality, write down a specific instance where this trait was clearly demonstrated. This could be a time when you overcame an obstacle, helped someone else, achieved a goal, or simply showed kindness to yourself.

_____
_____
_____
_____
_____
_____
_____

Affirmation Creation: Using the qualities and instances you've noted, create three personal affirmations. Format them in the present tense, starting with "I am" or "I have." For example, "I am resilient, as shown when I navigated through a difficult time by focusing on solutions and learning from the experience."

_____

_____

_____

_____

_____

_____

_____

_____

Daily Practice: Commit to repeating these affirmations to yourself daily, preferably in the morning or whenever you need a boost. You can say them out loud, write them in a journal, or even post them somewhere you'll see them regularly.

*Maintaining Resilience in the Face of Adversity*

The journey to manifesting your dreams is rarely a straight path. It's filled with twists, turns, and the occasional roadblock. The key to resilience is not the absence of failure but the persistence through it. Embrace each new beginning as an opportunity to apply what you've learned, to refine your approach, and to edge closer to your dreams with renewed strength and wisdom.

## Exercise: Opportunity Mapping

Let's develop the habit of identifying opportunities in every challenge, fostering an optimistic and growth-oriented mindset.

Challenge List: Write down three recent challenges or areas of your life where you're currently facing obstacles.

1. _____

2. _____

3. _____

Opportunity Brainstorm: For each challenge, brainstorm potential opportunities that could arise from these situations. Consider skills you might develop, knowledge you could gain, or new paths that might open up as a result.

1. _____

2. _____

3. _____
   _____
   _____

Action Steps: Choose one opportunity from each challenge and outline a concrete action step you can take to explore or take advantage of that opportunity. This step should be specific, measurable, and achievable.

1. _____
   _____
   _____

2. _____
   _____
   _____

3. _____
   _____

Review and Reflect: After a week, review your progress on these action steps. Reflect on any changes in your perception of the original challenges and any growth or insights gained through this process.

This exercise can help solidify your belief in obstacles as catalysts for growth.

Resilience doesn't mean you won't experience difficulty or distress. It means you'll handle such experiences in ways that foster strength and growth. Remember, resilience is like a muscle; it strengthens with use. Every challenge you face and navigate successfully builds your resilience, making you better equipped for future obstacles.

Viewing life's obstacles as opportunities and maintaining a positive self-esteem and attitude are not just strategies for building resilience; they're foundational principles for a fulfilling and purpose-driven life. By adopting these perspectives, you ensure that no matter how many times you may need to start over or try again, you remain steadfast in your journey toward becoming the person you've always dreamed of being.

Cultivating inner strength through resilience is essential for anyone looking to create a meaningful, fulfilling life. By developing resilience, you not only enhance your ability to manifest your desires but also enrich your journey with depth, wisdom, and an unshakeable sense of purpose.

**Reflective Questions:**

1. How do I typically respond to setbacks or challenges? How can I improve my response?
2. Reflect on a past challenge and write about how you overcame it. What strengths did you discover in yourself? What did you learn from the experience?
3. Identify areas where you feel you could improve your resilience. Set one specific, actionable goal for each area.
4. What positive affirmations can I use to reinforce my self-esteem when facing setbacks?
5. Who or what can I turn to for a dose of positivity and encouragement when I need it?

# Chapter 6:
# Harnessing the Power of Mindfulness and Presence

In the whirlwind of daily life, it's easy to lose ourselves in the noise, becoming disconnected from our true essence and the present moment. Mindfulness- the practice of being fully present and engaged with the here and now-offers a pathway back to connection, not just with ourselves but with the world around us. This chapter explores the transformative power of mindfulness and how cultivating presence can illuminate the path to becoming the best versions of ourselves.

*The Essence of Mindfulness*

Mindfulness is more than a practice; it's a way of being. It's about tuning in to the present moment with openness, curiosity, and without judgment. Whether you're eating, walking, or simply breathing, mindfulness invites you to experience each moment fully, without distraction or overthinking. This conscious presence allows you to witness the richness of life, reducing stress and enhancing your sense of well-being.

*Exercise: The Mindful Moment*

Choose a routine activity, such as drinking your morning coffee or walking to work. Engage in this activity with full attention. Notice the sensations, the sounds, the smells. If your mind wanders, gently bring it back to the present moment. Reflect on how this mindfulness practice impacts your experience of the activity and your mood.

_____
_____
_____
_____
_____
_____
_____

*Integrating Mindfulness into Daily Life*

Bringing mindfulness into your daily routine doesn't require hours of meditation. It's about small, intentional shifts in how you approach your day-to-day experiences, turning ordinary moments into opportunities for mindfulness.

*Exercise: Daily Mindfulness Integration*

~ Set three daily reminders to pause and take three deep, mindful breaths. Use these moments to ground yourself in the present.

~At the end of the day, jot down any observations or feelings about these moments of mindfulness in your journal.

*Mindfulness for Personal Growth*

Mindfulness is a powerful ally on your journey to self-discovery and personal growth. It helps you become more aware of your thoughts and feelings, recognize patterns, and make conscious choices that align with your true self.

*Exercise: Mindful Reflection*

~ Spend a few minutes each day in quiet reflection. Focus on your breath to center yourself, then allow yourself to reflect on your current thoughts and feelings.

~ Note any recurring themes or insights that arise, consider how these reflections can guide your personal growth journey.

*Overcoming Challenges with Mindfulness*

Mindfulness also offers a resilience tool when facing life's challenges. By staying present, you can navigate difficulties with a clearer mind and a calmer heart, responding rather than reacting.

## Exercise: Mindful Response Practice

~ Next time you encounter a stressful situation, take a moment to pause and breathe.

~ Observe your immediate thoughts and reactions without judgment. Consider if there's a more **mindful**, compassionate response you can choose.

**Reflective Questions:**

1. How has practicing mindfulness changed my daily experiences and interactions?
2. In what areas of my life can I benefit from more mindfulness?
3. What have I discovered about myself through mindful practices?

Mindfulness is a journey back to the essence of who you are. It's a practice that enriches your life, deepens your understanding of yourself, and enhances your interactions with the world. As you continue to explore and integrate mindfulness into your life, you open yourself to a world of presence, connection, and boundless potential.

# Chapter 7:
# Setting Boundaries and Overcoming People-Pleasing Behaviors

While being considerate and helpful is undoubtedly valuable, consistently prioritizing others' needs over your own can lead to a loss of self-identity and respect. Falling into the rhythm of people-pleasing can often lead us astray from our own path. This chapter is dedicated to understanding people-pleasing, recognizing its impact on your life, and guiding you through the process of setting boundaries and advocating for yourself.

*Understanding People-Pleasing*

At its core, people-pleasing is an adaptive behavior aimed at avoiding conflict and gaining approval. It's characterized by the constant need to meet others' expectations. Many people-pleasers aren't even aware of their tendencies, as these behaviors can be deeply ingrained from an early age. This relentless pursuit for external validation can stem from various factors, including low self-esteem, fear of rejection, or past experiences where our value was contingent on how much we could accommodate others.

The danger of people-pleasing lies not in the act of helping others but in the loss of personal agency and identity it often entails. This kind of behavior can often lead to a life of constantly neglecting your own needs, causing you to feel behind or stuck in life. Recognizing you're in this cycle is the first, vital step towards change.

If you're not sure if you are a pleaser, look for signs like struggling to say no, feeling responsible for others' happiness, and neglecting your own needs. Start by reflecting on moments where you felt drained or resentful after agreeing to something against your better judgment. What motivated your decision? Fear of conflict, guilt, or the need for acceptance? Identifying these patterns is crucial for understanding your people-pleasing behaviors and their triggers.

*Exercise: identifying People-Pleasing Patterns*

~ Reflect on recent instances where you prioritized someone else's needs or happiness over your own. What were the circumstances? How did you feel afterward?

~ Write down signs that indicate you're slipping into people-pleasing behaviors.

_____

_____

_____

_____

_____

_____

_____

## Letting Go of the Need to Always Be the "Nice Guy / Girl"

The need to always be perceived as nice or agreeable can trap you in a cycle of passiveness and dissatisfaction. Learning to discern when to step in and when to prioritize your peace is essential. Learning to let go of the incessant need to be liked or to avoid conflict is crucial for personal growth. Not every situation requires your sacrifice. Rationalizing when to assert yourself and when to let things go is key to maintaining your peace and self-respect. Remember, saying no and standing up for yourself doesn't take away from your kindness. You have to respect yourself and be kind to yourself too.

*Exercise: Rationalization and Response*

- Consider a time when your natural instinct was to agree for the sake of peace.

- Practice mentally stepping back and assessing: "Does this situation warrant my intervention, or am I acting out of obligation?" Learning to navigate these moments with your well-being in mind is a powerful step towards breaking the people-pleasing habit.

- Think of 3 times you've let someone push you around, or you went along with something you didn't agree with, simply for the sake of not causing waves. How did it make you feel in the moment? How did you feel afterwards?

_____
_____
_____
_____

_____
_____
_____
_____
_____
_____
_____
_____
_____

Next time you're inclined to automatically say yes or smooth over a situation, pause. Ask yourself: "Is this truly my responsibility? Am I compromising my well-being for the sake of peace?" Practice saying no in low-stakes situations to build your confidence in asserting your boundaries.

*Knowing Your Worth and Demanding Respect*

Your self-worth is not a currency for others' approval. Embracing this truth is liberating and forms the foundation for setting healthy boundaries. Asserting your needs and expecting respectful treatment is neither selfish nor demanding; it's a basic right. Understanding your worth is fundamental to setting boundaries and demanding the treatment you deserve. You do not have to tolerate disrespect or uncomfortable situations out of a misplaced duty to maintain harmony. Boundaries communicate your self-respect to others and teach them how you expect to be treated.

### Exercise: Self-Worth Affirmation

Create a list of affirmations that reinforce your worth and the right to respectful treatment. For example, "I deserve to be treated with respect," "My needs and feelings are valid," "I am not responsible for others' emotions."

_____

_____

_____

_____

_____

_____

_____

_____

Regularly remind yourself of these truths, especially when you feel pressured to compromise your boundaries.

### The Problem with Little White Lies

While little white lies may seem harmless, they're often a tool for avoiding discomfort at the moment, perpetuating the cycle of people-pleasing. Recognize that it's okay to say no without elaborate justifications. Honesty, even when it feels uncomfortable, fosters authenticity and respects both your time and that of others.

### Exercise: Honest Declines

Challenge yourself to decline requests without resorting to fabrications. A simple, "I won't be able to make it, but thank you for thinking of me," honors your commitments and models clear, respectful communication.

*Prioritizing Yourself*

Putting yourself first is not an act of selfishness; it's an act of self-respect. You are entitled to pursue your happiness and well-being with as much fervor as you lend to others' needs. Recognizing that your life is yours to shape frees you from the constraints of people-pleasing and opens doors to genuine self-expression and fulfillment. You have one life to live. It shouldn't be spent diminishing your light to let others shine brighter.

*Exercise: Self-Priority Plan*

Identify one activity each week that centers on your personal growth or joy-reading, meditation, or a hobby. This dedicated "me time" is a declaration of your worth and an essential practice in self-care. Reflect on how prioritizing yourself impacts your mood, self-esteem, and relationships.

_____

_____

_____

_____

_____

_____

_____

<u>Concluding Thoughts</u>

Overcoming people-pleasing isn't about becoming self-centered; it's about finding a healthy balance between kindness to others and kindness to yourself. By setting boundaries and prioritizing your well-being, you reclaim control of your life, ensuring that your generosity comes from a place of abundance and choice, not obligation or fear.

Transforming people-pleasing habits into a balanced life where kindness and self-respect coexist is a journey of many steps. It requires patience, self-compassion, and the courage to assert your worth. As you set forth on this path, remember that every step towards prioritizing your well-being not only enriches your life but also sets a profound example for those around you.

By embracing the practices and reflections outlined in this chapter, you're well on your way to shedding the weight of people-pleasing and stepping into a life marked by authenticity, self-respect, and genuine connections.

Remember, you are allowed to put yourself first. It's from this place of strength and self-respect that you can truly contribute to the world around you in meaningful ways.

## Chapter 8:
## Unleashing the Power Within: Manifesting Your Reality

Manifestation isn't just a mystical concept cloaked in mystery; it's a tangible, powerful process grounded in the principles of energy, intention, and the law of attraction. At its core, manifestation is the ability to bring into reality your desires and dreams through focused intention, belief, and action. This chapter aims to demystify the process of manifestation, explaining not only why it works but also how you can effectively implement it into your daily life to achieve profound changes and become the architect of your destiny.

*The Essence of Manifestation*

Manifestation is rooted in the understanding that everything in our universe is made up of energy, including our thoughts, emotions, and intentions. This energy vibrates at different frequencies, attracting similar frequencies in the process. The law of attraction, a key principle behind manifestation, assumes that like attracts like --- positive thoughts bring positive experiences, while negative thoughts bring negative outcomes. By aligning your thoughts and energy with what you wish to attract, you can bring about tangible changes in your life.

### Why It Works

The power of manifestation lies in its alignment with quantum physics and the understanding of the universe as an interconnected web of energy. When you focus your energy and intention on a specific goal or desire, you begin to attract circumstances, people, and opportunities that resonate with that same energy. This is not mere coincidence; it's the result of your active participation in shaping your reality through the energy you emit.

### Implementing Manifestation into Your Daily Life

Manifestation is more than occasional wishful thinking; it requires consistent, focused intention and belief in the possibility of achieving your dreams. Here are some foundational steps to integrate manifestation into your daily routine:

Clear Intention: The process of manifesting begins with clarity. You must be clear about what you want to achieve or bring into your life. This clarity of intention sets the foundation for your manifestation journey, as it guides your thoughts and actions toward your desired outcome.

Visualize and Embody: Spend time each day visualizing your desired outcome as if it has already happened. Embody the feelings and emotions associated with achieving your goal, as this enhances the vibrational match with your desire.

Affirmative Action: Use affirmations to reinforce your belief and commitment to your goals. Positive, present-tense affirmations can shift your mindset and open you up to receiving what you're working towards.

Mindful Awareness: Be mindful of your thoughts and emotions, steering them towards positivity and alignment with your goals. Remember, negative thoughts can detract from your manifestation efforts.

Gratitude: Cultivate a practice of gratitude. Being thankful for what you already have creates a positive energy flow and attracts more blessings into your life.

Letting Go: While it's important to be clear about your desires, it's equally crucial to let go of the outcome. Trust the process and be open to receiving what the universe has in store for you, even if it differs from your initial expectations.

## Exercise: Clarity of Intention

~ Spend some quiet time reflecting on what you truly desire in different areas of your life, such as personal growth, relationships, career, or health.

~ Write down your intentions, being as specific as possible. For each intention, ask yourself why it's important to you, as this will help to deepen your connection to your goals.

_____
_____
_____
_____
_____
_____
_____
_____
_____
_____
_____
_____
_____
_____
_____
_____
_____

## The Role of Mindset

Your mindset plays a crucial role in the manifestation process. A positive, growth-oriented mindset opens you up to the possibilities and opportunities necessary for achieving your goals. Conversely, a negative or limiting mindset can block these opportunities, keeping you stuck in patterns that don't serve your highest good.

---
*Exercise: Shifting Your Mindset*

---

~ Identify any limiting beliefs that might be holding you back from achieving your goals. These could be beliefs about your abilities, worthiness, or what you think is possible.

~ Challenge these beliefs by asking yourself if they're truly accurate. Replace them with empowering affirmations that reflect the reality you wish to create. For example, if you believe "I'm not good enough to achieve my dreams," replace it with "I am capable and worthy of achieving my dreams."

## Taking Inspired Action

While setting intentions and cultivating a positive mindset are key, manifestation also requires action. Inspired action is any step you take that feels aligned with your goals and intentions. It's about doing things that move you closer to your desired outcome, guided by intuition and a sense of purpose.

---

*Exercise: Planning Inspired Action*

---

~ For each of your intentions, list at least three inspired actions you can take to move closer to your goal. These actions should feel exciting and aligned with your values.

~ Schedule time to take these actions, and as you do, notice how taking aligned steps towards your goals creates momentum and brings your desires closer to reality.

*Cultivating Patience and Trust*

Manifestation is a process, and it often requires time, patience, and trust. Trusting in the timing of your life and maintaining faith in the process are essential components of successful manifestation.

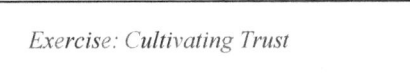

*Exercise: Cultivating Trust*

~ Practice mindfulness or meditation to connect with a sense of trust in the universe. Visualize your intentions coming to fruition, and feel the emotions associated with achieving your goals.

~ Whenever doubt creeps in, return to this practice to reaffirm your trust and maintain focus on your desired outcome.

*Tips for Better Manifestation*

Patience and Persistence: Manifestation is a journey, not a sprint. Be patient and persistent in your practices, understanding that timing plays a crucial role.

Alignment with Actions: Ensure your actions align with your goals. Manifestation works best when accompanied by steps that move you closer to your desired outcome.

Environmental Influence: Surround yourself with positivity and people who support your dreams and aspirations. Your environment can significantly impact your energy and manifestation ability.

For skeptics or those new to the concept, manifestation may seem like wishful thinking. However, when understood and applied with intention, belief, and action, it becomes a powerful tool for transforming your life. By adopting these practices and principles, you equip yourself with the ability to manifest not only what you desire but also to become the person you've always dreamed of being.

**Reflective Questions:**

1. What desires or goals am I most passionate about manifesting in my life?
2. What limiting beliefs do I need to release to create space for my desired reality?
3. How can I integrate inspired action into my daily routine to bring my intentions to life?

Manifestation is a powerful tool for creating the life you desire. By understanding and applying the principles of manifestation, you can tap into your inner power and transform your dreams into reality. Remember, the universe is always conspiring in your favor, and with clarity, intention, and action, you can manifest a life that reflects your truest desires.

## *Chapter 9:*

## *Creating a Life of Purpose and Meaning*

As you continue on your journey of self-discovery and growth, a pivotal moment arises when you start to question the deeper purpose of your life. What is it that gives your life meaning? How can you lead a life that not only fulfills you but also contributes to the world around you? This chapter is dedicated to exploring these profound questions, guiding you toward a life brimming with purpose and meaning.

*Discovering Your Purpose*

Your life's purpose is your unique contribution to the world, a blend of your passions, strengths, and the impact you wish to have. Finding your purpose is about tuning into your inner self and recognizing the values and passions that drive you.

*Exercise: Mapping Your Passions and Values*

Think of the activities that fill you with joy and satisfaction. Write down how these passions might translate into a purpose or mission.

_____

_____

_____

_____

_____

_____

_____

## Living with Intention

Leading a life of purpose means making choices that align with your sense of meaning and intention. It's about being deliberate in how you spend your time and energy, ensuring that your actions contribute to your broader goals.

*Exercise: Intention Selling*

Start each day by setting an intention that aligns with your purpose. Reflect on this intention throughout the day and evaluate your actions and decisions against it.

*Finding Meaning in Everyday Life*

Purpose is not only found in grand achievements but also in everyday moments. It's woven into the fabric of our daily lives through acts of kindness, moments of connection, and the pursuit of personal growth.

*Exercise: Daily Acts of Meaning*

Identify small actions you can take each day to live more meaningfully, such as helping someone, expressing gratitude, or learning something new. Then, reflect on the sense of purpose they brought you.

_____
_____
_____
_____
_____
_____
_____
_____
_____
_____
_____
_____
_____
_____

## Connecting with Others

Purpose often finds its fullest expression in connection with others. Whether through relationships, community involvement, or contributing to causes you care about, your purpose is amplified in the shared human experience.

---

*Exercise: Community Connection*

---

Identify a group, cause, or community where you feel drawn to contribute. Plan a small step you can take to engage with this community and integrate it into your pursuit of a meaningful life.

**Reflective Questions:**

1. How does my daily life reflect my purpose and values?
2. What small changes can I make to align more closely with my sense of meaning?
3. How do my connections with others enrich my pursuit of purpose?

Creating a life of purpose and meaning is an evolving journey, unique to each individual. This chapter offers a starting point for exploring what truly matters to you and how you can infuse your days with intention and fulfillment. As you move forward, remember that your purpose is a compass, guiding you through life's fluctuations with a sense of direction and hope.

## *Illuminating Your Path Ahead*

As we bring our journey to a close, remember, the essence of this book is not meant to be left behind on the last page. Rather, it's a beginning, a set of guiding principles to carry with you as you navigate the complexities of life. Through the chapters, we've ventured together through the landscapes of self-love, resilience, vulnerability, and authenticity. Each section was crafted to not only illuminate your path but also to equip you with the tools necessary for the journey ahead.

Standing now at the precipice of what's next, you are armed with knowledge and strategies that perhaps once seemed distant. The concepts we've explored together-embracing life's challenges as opportunities, fostering a deep-rooted sense of self, and walking your path with authenticity-are now woven into the fabric of your being.

This journey is inherently yours, unique and continuing. It's about embracing the inevitable setbacks as much as the victories, with the understanding that each step, forward or backward, is a part of your growth. The resilience and insight you've gained here are your companions as you move forward, guiding you through the fog of uncertainty to clearer vistas.

Your aspirations, the visions you have for your life, are within reach. With each page turned, you've built a foundation of belief in your ability to manifest these dreams into reality.
Trust in yourself and the process; the growth you seek unfolds in the actions you take each day, informed by the lessons you've learned.
Consider this book a touchstone on your journey-a source of inspiration and guidance as you carve out your path. The practices and reflections contained within these pages are not just for contemplation but for action, ready to be revisited as you grow, and your journey evolves.

As you step forward, remember that personal growth is a perpetual journey of becoming, filled with both challenges and triumphs. It's about continually aligning your actions with your deepest values and the vision, you hold for your life. You possess all the potential and strength needed to shape your life into a reflection of your most authentic self.

The path ahead is yours to shape, illuminated by the light of your own wisdom and courage. With the insights and tools, you've now embraced, you stand ready to face the future with confidence and a sense of purpose. Here's to moving forward, to growth, and to becoming the person you envision with every step you take.

# *Message from the Author*

This book is endorsed by Nightgod333 Secrets Revealed. Nightgod333 is an extraordinary creator who has captivated millions with his mind-blowing content. He challenges people to open their minds to new possibilities and reshape their understanding of reality, encouraging his followers to question everything and always seek the truth.

Nightgod333 has used the art of manifestation to transform his life and become the successful content creator he is today. He inspires his followers to believe in themselves and practice manifestation, emphasizing that no one should ever underestimate their capabilities. He advocates for never settling for less than you deserve and believes that with the right mindset, determination, and tools, anyone can manifest their dream life. This book is a great first step in that process.

Through self-exploration, you can discover what you truly desire and begin manifesting that desire. By using this book as a tool, you can start your journey to becoming the best version of yourself and living your best life.

Discover more at https://www.nightgod333.com, and join the community on Facebook at Nightgod333 Secrets Revealed.

*Journal Pages to Document Your Growth and Experiences:*

www.ingramcontent.com/pod-product-compliance
Lightning Source LLC
Chambersburg PA
CBHW071223160426
43196CB00012B/2401